STOP
unfinished business

FROM GOING TO
THE GRAVE

SETTLE THE ISSUE

Tips On How To Invest In Your Future & The Future Of Others

AUTHOR BETTIE CLAY

ISBN-10: 0615855423
ISBN-13: 978-0615855424

TABLE OF CONTENTS

Introduction

"God's word is a lamp unto our feet and a light unto our path." It is the light that we are expected to follow throughout our lives. The Bible is a written manuscript full of instructions. It doesn't leave one stone unturned. Our focus in this book is on relationships. As children of God, we must study the life of Christ and learn from it. When looking at His life, we clearly see that He finished what He started. There is no unfinished business in the Bible. The things that seem unfinished, He has made provision for them to be finished in the future. Our desire should be to model the life of Jesus each day. In this book, you will find tips that will help you settle issues, invest in your future as well as the future of others, and help you live a victorious life.

Relationships are important to the Lord and must become important to us. We must be willing to settle our differences before leaving this world. We must give honor where honor is due and we must forgive as Christ forgave us. The Father expects us to live a life that is pleasing to Him.

Stop

Unfinished

Business

Stop Unfinished Business

The word **stop** serves as a command, warning or suggestion. The definition means to cause, cease, or to cause to give up or change a course of action. Even though it would be easier to sing "I Surrender All", it is not quite so easy to give up or change what we were born in. According to scripture, we were born in sin, born in what displeases God, and born in unrighteousness, yet made in the image of God. It is obvious that what we were made in and born in are two different things. Being made in the image of God simply placed us in position to will and feel just as He does. This was part of his plan for man. Even though his plan for us was to be made in his image, the scripture also says "after his likeness" which would be an extension of his image.

Unfortunately not everyone chooses to pattern their life after him. While being in His image was an automatic, following after him is a choice. Anyone who makes the decision to follow Christ understands it's a choice and a process. We must choose to follow after his likeness. After God made man and man fell causing sin to enter the world this caused us to be born in sin; but Praise God that's not where the story ends! Because of God's love for us, He made provisions for us to have access to everything we would ever need to bring change in our lives. Now the sin that we were born in no longer holds us hostage and change is expected to take place in our lives. As a matter of fact change **must** take place. It's amazing how so many people say they're Christian and there's no change in their life. I realize some changes are gradual but they must be evident. The word Christian suggest we're to be Christ-like.

The Bible is the most inspiring book there is. I'm reminded of another scripture (Hebrews 12:1 that tells us to "lay aside every weight and the sin which so easily beset us….."). This scripture places the responsibility of ridding ourselves of any weight and sin that would trouble, harass, attack, or hinder us from moving forward and prospering in our relationships with God and people. Most of us deal with the sin in our lives but not the weight. Weights are the things that we tend to carry unnecessarily (things that are heavy and not easily moved). Weights can be the result of unresolved issues, marriage problems, and issues with our children or with others. Failing to understand the damage that weight can cause has caused some Christians to fall into sin. Weight has caused unresolved issues which have resulted in unforgiveness. We must understand that unforgiveness is one of the most popular poisons that the enemy uses against the people of God. Some people have been weighted down so long and feel there is no use thinking that their issues will never be resolved.

What has happened in the body of Christ is that we fail to reason together. As individuals we must find a way to obey the word of God. In James 1:15, we find that when sin is finished it bringeth forth death. Free yourself. Disobedience is sin.

So what is unresolved or unfinished business? Good question, and I'm glad you asked! Anything unresolved or unfinished is something that has been left undone. It is neither fixed nor finished. The saying is, if it ain't broke don't fix it. Some of the stuff that is broken we are not fixing and what is sad is some of it can be fixed and should be fixed. We would be surprised to know how many people throw away things that can be repaired. Is it because we do not want to invest the time, money, or effort to fix it? Is it easier to get a replacement? I'm sure that somebody would agree that getting a replacement is not always the right thing nor the wise thing to do.

Some find out later or when it is too late that they should have fixed it.

There are so many broken homes, relationships, and fellowships because no one would take the responsibility of attempting to fix whatever was wrong. Like Adam and Eve while in the garden pointing fingers at one another, no one wanted to take responsibility for their own actions and/or wrong doings. As believers we need to remember God does not hold you responsible for what someone does to you but for what you do or in some cases what you do not do concerning them. Whenever you know to do right and do not do it, you are in sin!

Our aim should be to live peaceably with all men whenever it is possible. When we trust God, He can make what seems or would be impossible, possible. As Christians we need to utilize everything that the Lord has made available to us. It appears that we have accepted the free ticket for salvation but we are not willing to work towards our spiritual growth. Many of us study the word of God but do not work out our own soul salvation. Remember it is a process.

Some Christians are still angry, holding grudges, hurt, jealous, weighted and have no peace. By not dealing with unfinished business it can cause you to die prematurely. Physically, spiritually, and emotionally some are already dead, dry, have no life or just existing. I applaud those like myself that have come close to dying and suddenly chose to live. There are some that came close to dying in their marriage, in family feuds, in friendships, finances and jobs but refused to die! We have got to learn to walk in victory in every area of our lives.

Serving God is a learned behavior. Learn to pray without ceasing because prayer changes things and people. Prayer can go where you cannot go and accomplish what needs to be done. Scripture tells us, God sent His word and it healed them. The word of God is so powerful and it accomplishes what it is sent out to do according to His will.

Who Told You Your Way Was the Right Way?

Who told you your way was the right way?

It is the enemy's job to deceive us, but our job is to measure our thoughts by the word of God. We have to be careful not to lean on our own understanding. Leaning on our own understanding is easy, convenient, but also dangerous. Most would agree that once a thought has been planted in our minds, we entertain it for days, weeks, months, and in some cases years. Whether we are right or wrong in our thinking, we continue to entertain it. What we fail to understand is once we begin to entertain the thought, we give life to it. The more we ponder on those thoughts, the more it takes root and the more we believe it. This can be dangerous because we seldom honestly consult the Lord. The Bible, clearly states "there is a way that seemeth right...". I find that we as people rely a lot on intellect, education, and other concepts to analyze situations, but we have to listen and abide by the word of God, which is truth. Too often we follow the thing that **seems** right.

When we compare what is right to what seems right we could have a different response. In some cases we should since there is a distinct difference between the two. Things that are right can be said and done with confidence. Wherein things that seem right we hesitate and show signs of uncertainty. Even though some are good at showing no outward signs of uncertainty, if they are a believer and the Spirit of God is active in their life they will not be comfortable.

The bible says, His sheep know His voice and in knowing His voice, they won't follow strangers. It is unbelievable how many of His sheep follow strangers because they are leaning on their own understanding and/or don't recognize His voice. When we don't seek Him, we tend to lean in the wrong direction and we stay wrong until we seek what is right. I believe, regardless of how convincing we sound to others, we know when we are wrong. I also believe we are wired to know right from wrong and good from evil. We may be able to fool people, but we will never be able to fool God. Something else that puzzles me about Christians, as prophetic as some Christians appear when something goes wrong, they seem not to be able to hear the voice of God. Would that be because they are not ready to receive the truth?

I am convinced that there is too much talk about God and His word and not enough of a lifestyle change in the hearers of the word. God's expectations of us are higher than what we are living.

Often we say we win in the end, I hope that statement is true. When I think about the word "win", a person would have played fair and adhered to all the rules of the game. In other words, all qualifications of the game were met and you would have stayed in the game until it ended. Regardless of how you felt about the game or what ideas you had, the rules of the game had already been set. When you decided to play the game, evidently you were willing to play according to the rules and not yours. The same holds true when we come to the Lord. We come on His terms and conditions not ours. When you made the decision to come, he expected you to abide by His rules because His way and His way ONLY is the right way. As long as we live, we are still learning to live holy. Therefore, we must be willing to kill our flesh, our will, and our way. There are times when situations may seem right, but that does not make it right.

"Who says your way is right?" is a good question. God asked Adam a similar question, "Adam who told you you were naked?" The catch here is to get you to think about where the idea originated, then maybe you will be able to determine if it is right or wrong. When questions are asked, they are asked to cause you to ponder on what is being presented. It is a fact that we consistently entertain negative thoughts when in all actuality what we are doing is entertaining what we should be ignoring.

There is no reason why a Christian should continue to entertain a lie or that which is wrong, or not true. Philippians 4:8-9 states, "Finally, brethren, whatsoever things are true, whatsoever things are honest, whatsoever things are just, whatsoever things are pure, whatsoever things are lovely, whatsoever things are of good report; if there be any virtue, and if there be any praise, think on these things." "Those things, which ye have both learned and received and heard and seen in me, do and the God of peace shall be with you." In these two verses, Paul sends a clear message of what we should be thinking and doing.

Let us agree that we are all emotional people. Regardless of whether our emotions run high or low, we have them and they do affect our behavior, moods, attitudes and actions. When we speak about being right, everybody should want to be right; right according to God's word and his way not according

17

to ours. The majority of the time our emotions get in the way which may cause us to be out of the will of God. When we do not control our emotions, they will certainly control us.

It is time that we do something for ourselves and a good place to start is by telling ourselves the truth. Truth allows us to be free. We tend to get upset when people talk to us about our ways because the truth hurts. Admitting the truth is the first step in our deliverance and healing process. We need to admit the truth. No one should have to tell you what you already know about yourself. The shame is not having issues, it is having them and not fixing them. Some of us do not want to deal with our own flesh, remember that others don't either. The Holy Spirit came to assist us, teach, lead, and guide us into all truths; even the truth about *you*! Let Him do it. The hardest thing to do is to get started. Now is a good time to start breaking old cycles in your life and changing your ways.

When Will Victory Be Mine?

When Will Victory Be Mine?

At what point do we stop living, acting and speaking defeat? So many of us live, act or speak as if we have no hope of victory. Whether we walk in victory or not as Christians, victory does belong to us. We have access to things that we refuse to accept, or we accept them in some areas and not in others. What causes our faith to soar in some areas and not in others? There could be many reasons but what is more important is not what you have done in the past but what are you going to do starting right now. It is an insult to God when we do not lay claim on the things that He has made available to us. It is important that we make Jesus our choice and victory too. Having Christ in your life and living in defeat in any area of your life is not a match. Some things just do not belong together.

Christians tend to look better on the outside but have major struggles and issues inside. We have been groomed to put the best on the outside but yet we are dying internally. Victory starts within. In some cases, we appear to be public successes and private failures. Again serving God is a learned behavior and some of what we learn is a result of what we have suffered. **Suffer** is not a bad word, it is considered a place of learning and a place where things work for your good. Psalms 119:71 states, "It is good for me that I have been afflicted; that I might learn thy statutes." Peter declared, "But the God of all grace, who hath called us unto (to share) his eternal glory by Christ Jesus, after that ye have suffered awhile make you perfect (complete), stablish (mature), strengthen (strong), and settle you."

Exodus 1:12 says, the more the people of God were afflicted the more they multiplied and grew. Victory tends to come with growth and growth comes in spurts. We often talk about growth spurts meaning we only see growth at certain stages of life. Generally, you experience growth spurts on or around a birthday. Birthdays are meant to show signs of growth and maturity. It is time that we overcome the struggles in our lives and walk in total victory!

So my question is when will you experience victory? The answer is when you come to a place of maturity and choose to walk in victory.

Who's the Blame Me or You?

Who's The Blame
Me or You?

Previously we mentioned how Adam and Eve blamed one another. Neither wanted to accept responsibility for the fall and certainly there has not been much change from then to now. There are some things we are just good at and playing the blame game is one of them. The blame game is found in all ages and races, it is found in high places, among family members and friends. The game is even played in the church, on the job, and everywhere. Siblings play it quite often. Taking responsibility is just not something people like to do. In most cases what we do not like to do are things we should be doing and vice versa.

Paul in Romans 7:18 – 19 says, "For I know that in me (that is, in my flesh) dwelleth no good thing: but how to perform that which is good I find not." "For the good that I would I do not: but the evil which I would not, that I do." If you will allow me to borrow from this text just to prove that what we normally do is not what we should be doing nor what we like to do. We like saying I am only human or this runs in the family. We like excuses, but there are times we are without excuse. Paul talks about his previous struggle but before he talked about his struggle, Paul said, for I know that in me, that in my flesh dwelleth nothing good. If we know there is nothing good in our flesh then it becomes our responsibility to seek what we need to perform that which is good. The bible says, if we seek we'll find, but at what point do we stop operating out of our flesh? Flesh is a mess and prevents us from receiving God's best. Regardless of what area of struggle Paul was talking about, the principle here is the same. We struggle but how long in the same area? I agree that some areas of struggle are more difficult than others but we can never stop reaching for deliverance.

Never give up on what God is able to do and he wants to do it through you! We should never blame anyone else for our behavior. Remember God knows all things even what is in our hearts and as far as who is to blame. Well, sometimes it's "Me" and sometimes it is "You." It depends on what side you're on. When you're talking to yourself you'll probably say it's "me" but if you look at yourself in the mirror you'll probably refer to yourself as "you." Either way the blame is on "me" or "you", both being the same person. Take responsibility for your actions!

Instructions for the Family

Instructions for the Family

The book of Ephesians is a good book for instructions. It speaks to the family. It speaks to the body of Christ and directly to husbands, wives, and children. It takes us on a love walk; a walk that encourages us to do what is right. It instructs us on what to put off, what to put on, and what to put away. It also instructs us to be followers of God and to walk in love.

The book of Ephesians can also be seen as a challenge. In reading it you will discover how good you are at following instructions.

In Chapter 5, Paul speaks to wives and husbands about submission and love. The wife is to reverence her husband and the husband is to love his wife as Christ loved the church. However, love and respect are expected to be demonstrated by both parties. As

Christ loved the church, he gave himself as a sacrifice. In verse 26 the purpose of this sacrifice is clear, that he might sanctify and cleanse it. This cleansing is a necessary process in getting the church ready to be presented to Him without spot or wrinkle. His intent is for the church to look like Him and His aim is to make us one. He is the head and we are the body. And together we are better.

If we follow these instructions, we would have fewer divorces. Building relationships takes time. It is a process that requires submission, giving, and taking. In most cases, it can be done with the help of the Lord, but He requires you to ask for help. He is always willing to help those that are willing to decrease and allow Him to increase.

Ephesians is definitely proof that God is for families. In Chapter 6, He speaks to the children. His instructions to them are to obey their parents and honor both father and mother. The promise for their obedience is that things may be well with them and that they have long life. In verse 4 there is a note to the father. He is instructed to provoke not his children to wrath but train them in the things of the Lord. What we must understand is that we are in the family of God and we must follow the instructions of our heavenly father. Is there a possibility that the

"Father" is disappointed in you?

Remember, obedience is key. Some situations can be avoided if you obey. We must obey someone and the one person we are all expected to obey is the Lord. The Bible is full of commands and instructions to be carried out by His children. Love is not something you speak, it is what you do. If we love Him, we will do what He says!

Giving Honor Where Honor Is Due

Giving Honor where Honor is Due

Honor comes from within and it is shown outwardly. Much like love, honor is demonstrated. It has a way of identifying itself. To honor someone does not mean you agree with them or like what they do. It means you respect their decisions, honor their requests, and their position.

The Bible, being the bestselling book ever, and the Holy Spirit, being the best author, deserves to be read over and over again. There are so many words, topics, and subjects that require our attention. Even though reading is important, I find it more amazing when the Holy Spirit begins to speak to me concerning the things close to His heart.

As Christians, it is important that we have ears to hear what the Spirit is saying to us, the church. The Lord is requiring us to give honor where honor is due. Some find it easier to give honor at the courthouse, work, school, etc. Some find it easier to give or show honor to other people and exemplify it in certain places but we miss the mark when we do not honor God and/or His people. Therefore, this puts us in the category of being a hypocrite. Scripture says, what you do unto the least of my little ones, you do it as unto me. Make sure you honor God in word and deed.

We must not forget that charity starts at home. Home is where the heart is. Let us not forget the bridge that brought you across, and whatever you do, do not burn it just yet. You may need it again. In talking about bridges, we are speaking of the different people that the Lord uses to get us from point A to point B in life. And He, being God, uses whomever He pleases. God's will can be amazing.

Exodus 20:12 states, "Honor thy father and thy mother, that thy days may be long upon the land which the Lord thy God giveth thee." This scripture has always been considered the first commandment with a promise and is just as important as any other. If we are not giving honor where honor is due, we are not pleasing God.

Let us take a closer look at Exodus 20:12. "Honor thy father and thy mother." The beginning of this passage is the command and the promise comes later. We must be careful not to put the cart before the horse, as we so often do. **Honor** according to Webster means, respect and esteem shown to another. It is safe in this case to say that the word **another** refers to our mother and father. This may get touchy, but it needs to be addressed, especially in this hour where respect is hard to find. Some parents may seem to be out of place, looking and acting like their children, but be mindful that the Bible is clear on the fact that they are still due honor.

I have never seen so many disrespectful children than what I see today. I am not just speaking of young or teenage children, but adult children as well. It is amazing to me as I think back on how so many children had the opportunity to go to college with the help of at least one parent. They now have decent jobs and seem to be doing well, but, how many of them fail to say THANK YOU? Thank you can be said in so many ways since actions speak louder than words.

I believe the lack of honor given and love shown to parents is causing their bodies to be diseased and their lives to be shortened. When was the last time you spent time with your parents, told them how much you love them or prepared a meal and invited them to your home? How many times have you used a bad choice of words or raised your voice to them because now you are *grown*?

Understand the command comes with no ifs, ands, or buts. Honor your father and your mother. Whether your father is the neighborhood drunk and your mother has had six children by six different men. Guess what? They are still due honor.

I remember when my mom, who was my best friend, passed away. When she passed, I wanted so badly to purchase a headstone for her grave. Unfortunately, I was not able to do so at the time. After being in a car accident and receiving a settlement, I was able to purchase the headstone. The Lord spoke to me saying He would bless me because I honored her even in her death. To understand the reasoning behind this you would have had to have known my mother. In her mind she would think she deserved a headstone. She would have said, "After all I've done for you, you mean to tell me you couldn't get me a headstone!" I am not telling any of you that teeth and tongue will not disagree at times, however if you want your days to be long upon the land, you must give honor to both mother and father.

Whatever you do, do not let the sun go down on your wrath. There is entirely too much unfinished business either in the family or in the grave. Wherever it is, get it right. God is holding you responsible. We cannot make anyone change their minds nor make them hear or accept what we say. As my mom used to say, "There's more than one way to skin a cat." Write a letter, send flowers, ask for forgiveness and mean it. Don't give up! When all else fails, pray until something happens. God answers prayers. Remember, the enemy wants to divide families because where there is unity, there is strength.

Proverbs 23:22 states, "Hearken unto the father that begat thee and despise not thy mother when she is old." Hearken means to give respectful attention; to give heed to, to hear. To give ear, listen. Again, we cannot get away from honor. Proverbs also encourages us to listen and pay attention to the father; the one who begat thee or was responsible for your being here. Often we say, "If it had not been for the Lord, I don't know where I'd be." This is definitely a true statement.

We also see another side in Proverbs, if it were not for your father, you would not be here. It goes on with further instructions, and despise not thy mother when she is old. The word despise means to look down with contempt or aversion and to regard as negligible, worthless, or distasteful. So again, we need an ear to hear what the spirit is yet saying to us.

We need to care for our parents in their old age; it will not be as long as they cared for us. They were responsible for us at least eighteen years. We need to seriously consider serving them since most of us will have no problem benefiting from their inheritance. Honor your father and mother so *their* days can be long upon the land too! Honoring them helps them to live longer and have more fruitful lives. There is too much unfinished business in the grave.

We have talked about our natural parents, but something should be said of the importance of honoring our spiritual parents as well. Disrespect has not only hit our homes, but the church as well. The Bible tells us to study to show ourselves approved. This is a necessity. Studying helps to eliminate ignorance, but here again the concepts that seem to be most important are the things that we neglect the most.

Studying, prayer, and giving are three of the most neglected aspects in the church. We also fail to honor the men and women of God. Some feel that because we all put our pants on the same way, we are all equal. Equal as men and women, but not in rank. Regardless of what field we are in, there is always a hierarchy. There would be too many wild bucks if there was no one appointed to lead. When we begin to study and understand God's word, we understand that honor is due your leader too!

1 Timothy 5:17 "Let the elders who rule well be counted worthy of double honor, especially they who labor in the word and doctrine."

Hebrews 13:17, "Obey them that have the rule over you, and submit yourselves: for they watch for your souls, as they that must give account, that they may do it with joy, and not with grief; for that is unprofitable for you."

How our actions influence...

How our actions influence our children and those around us

Let us analyze two popular quotes: "Action speaks louder than words" and "People can't hear what you say for watching what you do." Both statements are true. Therefore, we have to be careful of what we are doing. For those that are parents, God has given us an awesome responsibility. He trusted us with this leadership role making us responsible for leading, guiding, teaching, and training our children. They are considered our children because God entrusted us with them. However, not only are we responsible for them but we owe it to everyone around us and even those we come in contact with, to be good leaders.

It is a known fact that what people see has more of a lasting impression. Unfortunately, I have seen children damaged over the years because of something their parents had done or something that had taken place in the family that trickled down through the family causing a separation for generations. Please understand, this is not the will of God. We must admit that Jesus was our perfect example in everything and we are without excuse when we do not follow His lead.

Some would love to say, you do not understand or you do not know my family. That is correct, but nor do I need to. Even though you know them, you should know God's word better. You should know there is nothing too hard for Him and that He specializes in things that *seem* impossible. Also, be mindful of those that the Lord has placed around you. They are there not to be damaged or destroyed, but that we would be the Christian example that God requires us to be. One of the most popular slogans, "WWJD (What Would Jesus Do) " was actually a good saying and we might want to consider it from time to time. If we do what He did, we will be okay.

When we make bad choices in life, we can rest assure that somebody will be affected by them. All children need to experience love and happiness in the home, then hopefully they will practice the same philosophy outside of the home. In the event that they do not, it will not be your fault. Remember, in our role as leaders, we can cause people to live or die. Maybe not die physically, but spiritually, emotionally, and mentally.

Our children are our fruit. No one puts the time and effort into the growth of fruit and then destroy it. Just as farmers water, cultivate, feed, and nurture their crops because it is an investment to them, we are expected to do the same. If we invest in our children's future ultimately everyone will be blessed. The Proverbs 31 woman was blessed and her family called her blessed. Because of her blessings, they were all blessed.

Quality Time

Quality Time

As Christians we have our time of devotion. We pray, read, and meditate on the word of God. We like to think of this time as quality time.

Consequently, it may or may not be when looking at the word "quality". We find it deals with a certain degree of excellence, in order for us to spend quality time with the Lord we will need to clear our minds of the residue of yesterday's clutter.

Also noting, anything of quality is not only important but in some cases, necessary. Usually these things are lasting and causes us to receive the best service out of its use. Quality time should also be time invested in the Kingdom of God causing us to receive a return.

Unfortunately, when we pick up the Bible or kneel to pray, our minds are not always on what we are supposed to be doing. This is not quality time since the time is not being used for what it is intended for. Time can be classified in three categories: quality, quantity, and quiet time. Whenever you are spending quality time, usually quantity and quiet times are present. Quality time is known to usher in quantity and quietness of time. Quality time needs them because together they are more effective. Understand quality time is an indication that you recognize the importance of what you are doing and see the benefit it will bring.

It is also important that we understand when time is not used wisely there may be consequences. There is a great possibility that goals will be delayed or never reached. Misuse of time may also cause us to live life with regrets or saying what we could've, should've or would've done. To avoid any of this let us focus on the importance of quality time.

Time is a Valuable Asset

Time is a Valuable Asset

Time has its advantages and disadvantages. There are times it can work for you or work against you. We would like to think that time is on our side, but as we take notice today, the days are getting shorter and shorter; causing the days, weeks, months, and years to pass very quickly. As we look at time, we probably would agree that it should not be taken lightly, nor should it be wasted. We can never replace time, making it that much more valuable.

In looking at Ecclesiastes 3:1, we see time classified in seasons. The passage reads, "To everything there is a season, and a time to every purpose under the earth. . ." Everything has a time frame and a frame of time for every purpose. In essence, our time is limited and we do not have time to waste. Unfortunately, we are all guilty at some point in our lives of wasting time. Some of us have had regrets because of this.

Wasted time has also caused a lot of unfinished business to be in the grave. If there are unresolved issues in your life, you may need to handle them while there is still time. Isaiah 1:18 -20 says, "Come now, and let us reason together, saith the Lord." Notice here it says come *NOW*. Why now? Because later may be too late. Verse 19, "If ye be willing and obedient, ye shall eat the good of the land." This verse speaks of the reward for obeying the instructions in verse 18. Verse 20, "But if you refuse and rebel, ye shall be devoured with the sword: for the mouth of the Lord has spoken it." This is the consequence for disobeying the instructions in verse 18. It is amazing how one word such as *NOW* can carry so much weight. In some cases coming now versus coming later can make a huge difference. Just as the time it takes to get someone from home to the hospital can determine whether they live or die.

Come now, resolve your issues. Set your house in order and prepare to meet Jesus when He comes. Preparation must be done in many areas of our lives. Remember, time is valuable.

If There's Life, It's Not Too Late

If There's Life, It's Not Too Late

As much as the enemy wants us to think that unfinished business cannot be resolved or that it is too late or that there is no hope, it is a lie. As often as we wished we would have handled some things differently, it is still not too late. Thank God for His grace and mercy; His willingness to allow us to come boldly to His throne to obtain mercy and find grace to help in a time of need.

There are times that it seems impossible to make contact with an individual in whom we have had a disagreement with. They may even be deceased, but even in those circumstances, it is important to clear your end with the Lord. If it cannot be settled with them, settle it in you, and with the help of the Lord, you can be free. God's grace and mercy is available to us in our times of need. That is good news! Even though the situation may seem hopeless, the outcome can be a healing experience for you. God's word always offers us a way of escape from bondage to freedom.

It is important that we refuse to entertain Satan's lies. Do not entertain those things that should be ignored and when possible do not allow the sun to go down on your wrath.

How

far are you

willing to go...

How far are you willing to go and how much are you willing to pay?

In determining how far we are willing to go we must first understand that following after God has never been easy, but having His word and his spirit is intended to make it possible. Living holy and living righteous lives is possible and easier when we see its value. I believe it is safe to say that things seem to have more value when there is a cost involved or you have worked hard to earn it. A great example is our children. They normally do not value their belongings because they did not have to earn the money that purchased the items. It is the same issue with the utilities. They leave the lights on throughout the house and constantly adjust the heat. They do not have to pay the bills. They lose valuable belongings or loan them to others, and without hesitation, they ask for more. At this point in their lives, these things carry little or no value.

In some cases, we may react the same way in relationships with people and with God. Even though relationships are said to be for a reason, a season, or for a lifetime, they are all important. There is still purpose for all of them. Seasons change, but the reason should always be valued. There is a reason for all seasons.

Relationships are important. If for no other reason, they are important because everyone needs somebody sometime. No man is an island, nor is it good for man to be alone. God Himself did not want to be alone.

Maybe in understanding the importance of relationships, we will value them more. Relationships require work. The more you work at them and work on them, the more valuable the relationship becomes. Things are more valuable after you have invested a lot of time and effort into them. You do not easily give up. Instead, you are more willing to stand up for what is right in the sight of God and tell that which is truth even when it is the truth about you.

How far are you willing to go and how much are you willing to pay? Jesus went all the way to the cross. He died that we might live. Are you willing to die that someone else can live a longer, healthier and happier life? Are you willing to accept the challenge of God's word? Will you settle the unresolved issues in your life? Will you stop unfinished business from going to the grave?

So
What Now?

So What Now?

In reading and studying God's word, there are some things that stand out more than others: **faith, love** and **obedience.** According to the Bible, without faith, it is impossible to please God. The word impossible is a strong word and carries a significant amount of weight.

Love, defined by Webster, is an affection based on admiration or benevolence. This seems to be an indication that love is based on how we feel, what we see, how we are treated or what we receive. But for God, who is love, love is demonstrated out of His nature without feelings, gifts, or actions. Even though there are benefits for those that love Him and obey His word, His love for them is not based on their actions toward Him.

As Christians, love should emanate out of us as proof that Christ lives in us. Unfortunately, as Christians we are still missing the mark. In this very moment, I suggest we pause and think about where we would be or what condition we would be in if the Lord had not extended His love toward us when he did.

The world still needs love. Love is important because it is the root cause of what Jesus did for us. The Bible says He knew no sin, but became sin for us, only because He loved us and desired to obey His father.

We are expected to obey God's word which states, "If you love me, keep my commandments," (John 14:15).

I am encouraging you today to deal with your emotions, and bring them under control so that you can live a happy healthy life in Christ.

All scripture quotations are from the King James Version (KJV), copyright © 1976, Thomas Nelson, Inc., Publishers, unless otherwise noted.

All definitions are from the Webster's Seventh New Collegiate Dictionary, A Merriam-Webster. Based on Webster's Third New International Dictionary.

Bettie Clay Ministries
P. O. Box 38733
Charlotte, NC 28278

Stop Unfinished Business from Going to the Grave
Settle the Issue
ISBN-10: 0615855423
ISBN-13: 978-0615855424

Printed in the United States of America
Cover Design by TC Design Solutions (704) 971-7854

About the Author

Bettie Clay, a native of Philadelphia, PA currently resides in Charlotte, NC. She has one daughter and two wonderful grandchildren. Bettie's voice is full of wisdom and truth which has been instrumental in the lives of many that she has come in contact with over the years. She has been in ministry for over 32 years. She founded and pastored for 11 years and currently oversees Refuge House of God Deliverance Ministries.

Being unctioned by the Lord, Bettie believes this book will be a blessing to you as she writes from life experiences and with the wisdom of the Lord.

www.ingramcontent.com/pod-product-compliance
Lightning Source LLC
Chambersburg PA
CBHW071734020426
42331CB00008B/2022